Rise and Shine

Elda Cadogan

A Samuel French Acting Edition

SAMUELFRENCH.COM
SAMUELFRENCH-LONDON.CO.UK

Copyright © 1984 by Elda Cadogan
All Rights Reserved

RISE AND SHINE is fully protected under the copyright laws of the United States of America, the British Commonwealth, including Canada, and all other countries of the Copyright Union. All rights, including professional and amateur stage productions, recitation, lecturing, public reading, motion picture, radio broadcasting, television and the rights of translation into foreign languages are strictly reserved.

ISBN 978-0-87440-555-2

www.SamuelFrench.com
www.SamuelFrench-London.co.uk

For Production Enquiries

United States and Canada
Info@SamuelFrench.com
1-866-598-8449

United Kingdom and Europe
Plays@SamuelFrench-London.co.uk
020-7255-4302

Each title is subject to availability from Samuel French, depending upon country of performance. Please be aware that *RISE AND SHINE* may not be licensed by Samuel French in your territory. Professional and amateur producers should contact the nearest Samuel French office or licensing partner to verify availability.

CAUTION: Professional and amateur producers are hereby warned that *RISE AND SHINE* is subject to a licensing fee. Publication of this play(s) does not imply availability for performance. Both amateurs and professionals considering a production are strongly advised to apply to Samuel French before starting rehearsals, advertising, or booking a theatre. A licensing fee must be paid whether the title(s) is presented for charity or gain and whether or not admission is charged. Professional/Stock licensing fees are quoted upon application to Samuel French.

No one shall make any changes in this title(s) for the purpose of production. No part of this book may be reproduced, stored in a retrieval system, or transmitted in any form, by any means, now known or yet to be invented, including mechanical, electronic, photocopying, recording, videotaping, or otherwise, without the prior written permission of the publisher. No one shall upload this title(s), or part of this title(s), to any social media websites.

For all enquiries regarding motion picture, television, and other media rights, please contact Samuel French.

Please refer to page 25 for further copyright information.

CHARACTERS

PHILIP SANDFORD GRANT
HEPZIBAH MERCY JONES
HENRY JOSEPH JONES
JANE MORRISON JONES

The time is dawn on a summer morning.

The place is Willowdale Cemetery, Jones Falls.

RISE AND SHINE

THE SETTING: When the curtain rises the audience finds the stage in utter darkness. Just when they begin to think nothing will happen, off-stage a trumpet bursts into a wild, rapturous, definitely "come hither" summons. From the darkened stage comes a rushing, scuffling sound; the audience half sees, half senses, that many people are quickly and noisily leaving the stage. Then there is silence and the utter darkness lifts a little; a half light fills the stage. The audience sees that they are in a cemetery. As many graves as the stage will hold are placed at intervals. The headstones are of various shapes and sizes and they are overturned, revealing what appear to be yawning holes. But no, wait a minute! They are not all overturned. At the front, to the right, stands one marker undisturbed, and half way back, to the left, stands another. When the audience has had time to observe this, the headstone to the right, front, begins to quiver. It does a sort of anguished little dance, lurching, right, left, backward and forward and finally topples with a crash.

PHILIP emerges, yawning and rubbing his eyes. His wearing apparel is rather odd, to say the least. At the front he is wearing what appears to be a very correct black coat, an immaculate collar and a somber tie. But when he turns around, the audience sees that the coat is only a dummy for the back is of a very shoddy factory cotton. Below the waist his dress is even more inadequate for he wears a pair of striped shorts and black socks, but no shoes. In spite of this rather extraordinary clothing, Philip presents an attractive, rather rakish appearance. PHILIP puts a hand tentatively toward his head and then rubs one arm slowly. He looks about him, dazed, with an air of bewilderment.

PHILIP. What happened to me? *(He rubs his head, swivels his neck around loosely, side to side, forward and back)* I certainly must have tied one on. Where in blazes have I got to? Looks for all the world like a cemetery. My God, it is a cemetery! Is this somebody's idea of a joke? *(He catches sight of his own headstone. He reads)* "Philip Sandford Grant, born August 3, 1958, died September 15, 1984." Good God! *(Realizing his situation)* I'm dead. Good G-G-Gosh, I mean, I'm dead! *(He sits down on headstone, head in hands)* Now, Philip, old boy, let's not get excited. Let's keep calm. Let's think things through. *(Excited again)* Dead! Dead! Me, of all people! *(Calmer)* What in the world was I doing last? Where was I? I seem to remember something about a car ... and there was a tree — I'm practically certain there was a tree in there somewhere, all leafy. Did I come a cropper, d'you suppose? *(A sudden thought strikes him)* Good Lord, I borrowed Bill's car. What will he say? *(He leaps up, then sinks down dejectedly)* Whatever he said, I guess he's said it by this time. Say, I wonder how long I've been dead? Headstone looks a bit weathered. No flowers around. And how did I get out? *(He begins to observe other graves)* Why, look. Everybody's out. They're all gone. Looks as though there's been a grave robbers' convention. But why am *I* still here? *(He runs first to one side of the cemetery, then to the other, peering out. He comes back, shaking his head. He sits down again. Suddenly he becomes conscious of his clothes. He leaps up in horror, with a shrinking motion and an attempt to cover his lower region with his hands)* Good heavens! What kind of an outfit is this I'm wearing? Where are my pants? What if somebody should come? *(He pulls headstone up and places it in front as a shield)* How could they do this to me? It was good old brother Bill, I'll bet. He always was a penny-pincher. And I'll bet he's wearing my pants right this minute! Lord, I wish I knew how to haunt him. *(He puts headstone down and sits on it)* Well, Philip, you've been and gone and done it this time and no mistake. Can't go anywhere dressed like this. Don't know where I am, anyway. Must be old Willowdale cemetery, I guess. If I go home there's apt to be a devil of a row. Like to see old Bill's face when I walk in, though. Well, the only thing to do is wait until dark and sneak home. Boy, wouldn't I like to jump out at Bill and yell, "Where're my pants?" *(He puts his head in his hands. There is silence for a few seconds. Then, from the direction of the other tombstone still standing comes a feminine voice, gentle and sweet and very sleepy)*

HEPZIBAH. H-e-e-n-r-y!

PHILIP. *(He jumps as though shot. He pulls the headstone in front of him with frantic haste and looks anxiously in the direction of the voice)* What was that? Sounded like a woman! Wonder if I can get back in my grave? *(He drops the headstone, falls to his knees and begins to dig furiously with his hands like a dog)*

HEPZIBAH. *(Calling louder)* H-e-e-e-n-r-y!

PHILIP. *(Looking toward other grave)* Sounds as though it was coming from that grave. Good grief! That headstone is still standing. Sounds as though there's a woman in there. Pants or no pants, I'm going to take a look. *(He tiptoes over with exaggerated care. Reads headstone)* Hepzibah

Mercy Jones. Here lies Hepzibah Mercy Jones who died at the birth of her sixth daughter, June 1, 1884, in her twenty-fifth year. "By their fruits ye shall know them." Ha! That's a good one! Died 1884. That makes her 125 years old. Pretty moldy by this time, I guess. Well, Philip, that's your luck, my boy. Stuck in a cemetery, without your pants, with a woman 125 years old!

HEPZIBAH. *(Imperative)* Henry!

PHILIP. *(Nervously)* Yes, er — ah — Hepzibah?

HEPZIBAH. Tell me quickly, was it a boy or a girl?

PHILIP. *(With a quick look at the headstone)* A girl.

HEPZIBAH. *(Sadly)* Oh, Henry, I am sorry. I did try, truly I did. I tried and tried and tried. I'm as anxious to carry on the name of Jones as you are.

PHILIP. *(Awkwardly)* That's all right, my dear.

HEPZIBAH. I'm so deliciously sleepy. I don't ever want to get up again. But I suppose I'd better try.

PHILIP. *(Alarmed)* No! No! You just rest. Don't try to get up.

HEPZIBAH. But Henry, you know how helpless you are with the children. *(She rises from her grave, a pretty young woman clad in a long white flannelette nightgown, very full, and fastened with ribbons at the wrists. She wears a frilly cap on her curly hair. At sight of Philip she screams. She tries to cover herself with her hands. PHILIP tries to cover himself. They are a pitiful pair. She screams again)*

PHILIP. Now, now Hepzibah, please don't scream like that. I can explain everything if you'll just listen. You see, you've been dead for a hundred years... *(HEPZIBAH screams again, backing away)* Please stop screaming, I won't hurt you. I'm dead too, and... *(HEPZIBAH faints. PHILIP is frantic. He rubs her wrists and head. He shouts)* Help! Help! There's a dead woman here and she's fainted. Somebody help me. Oh, what a mess! What in the world am I going to do? *(HEPZIBAH opens her eyes slowly, gets up and leans weakly against him. He leads her to the bench downstage and seats her. He sits beside her, still rubbing her hands)* That's a girl. Just rest now. Don't worry about a thing. Everything is just fine. *(He pats her)*

HEPZIBAH. But... You said I was dead.

PHILIP. Well, as a matter of fact — now, don't scream again, — you *are* dead. *(HEPZIBAH moans. She puts her head down on his shoulder)* Now, don't be frightened. It's all right. It doesn't hurt a bit. Be a brave girl.

HEPZIBAH. Oh, I'm so mixed up. Where's Henry? Why are you dressed like that? What is this awful place I'm in? Surely it isn't Heaven? Or is it Hell? Did God really give me black marks for all those thoughts I had about Henry?

PHILIP. Please don't try to talk, Hepzibah. And don't go worrying about things. I'm pretty muddled up myself. I only found out I was dead a few minutes ago. I know men are supposed to be brave and all that, but you might as well know I feel pretty shaky, too. So don't go screaming and fainting any more. I can't stand it.

HEPZIBAH. But you said you'd explain everything.

PHILIP. Well, here's the way I've got it figured out. If I'm on the right track, this is Willowdale Cemetery in Jones Falls and it's summer and daylight and the year is sometime after 1984.

HEPZIBAH. You mean 1884.

PHILIP. No. Now, you've got to face it sooner or later,

Hepzibah, and screaming and fainting won't help. You are at least 125 years old.

HEPZIBAH. You are mad! You are absolutely mad!

PHILIP. No, I'm not. I know it isn't a pleasant surprise for a girl to find out she's 125. It wasn't a pleasant surprise for me. I like them younger, myself. But calling names won't change it. It's right on your headstone that you died in 1884 and it's on mine that I died in 1984 so that's final.

HEPZIBAH. *(Beginning to cry softly)* I just can't think. My head is going round and round. I used to worry and worry about getting to be thirty. Just five more girls to go, I used to think, and I'll be thirty. And now you say I'm a hundred and twenty-five.

PHILIP. Please don't cry. It makes me nervous. Besides my handkerchief's in my pants pocket and I don't know where my pants are. This is the way my own family buried me. Cheapskates! At least you're decently covered.

HEPZIBAH. But this is my nightgown! And you're a strange man and you're *not* decently covered, and oh, I don't know what Henry is going to say. *(She wipes her eyes on her nightgown sleeve)*

PHILIP. What Henry's going to say is the least of my worries at the moment.

HEPZIBAH. If this is a cemetery, where are the others?

PHILIP. Do you know what I think?

HEPZIBAH. What?

PHILIP. I think we've missed the resurrection!

HEPZIBAH. Oh, no!

PHILIP. Well, that's what I think. You know, now that my head is clearing a little, it seems to me I remember hearing a horn.

HEPZIBAH. You mean ... Gabriel?

PHILIP. It must have been. *(They stare at each other)*

HEPZIBAH. But why didn't we hear him? Why didn't we go with the others?

PHILIP. I don't know yet. Mother always said I'd sleep through Judgment Day. I thought it was a joke, but now it doesn't seem so very funny.

HEPZIBAH. And I was so tired, those last few months, I used to fall right out of my chair, sound asleep. I used to say... *(She stops, her hand up to her mouth)* I used to say I'd like to sleep a hundred years. *(The look at each other, awestricken)*

PHILIP. *(Simply)* Well, that's it. We slept in.

HEPZIBAH. Henry is going to be awfully angry. He always says I haven't any more sense than a chicken. He says I'm always doing the silliest things. *(Sighing)* Wait till he finds out about this!

PHILIP. Henry sounds pretty disagreeable.

HEPZIBAH. *(Guiltily)* Oh, I shouldn't talk like that about Henry. He's a good man. And I really am a bit flighty. Henry makes me nervous. And the girls upset him. They're all like me.

PHILIP. Hepzibah, I don't like to worry you any more, but there's one thing that doesn't seem to have occurred to you.

HEPZIBAH. What's that?

PHILIP. Well, if you've been dead for a hundred years, I guess Henry must be dead, too.

HEPZIBAH. You mean ... I'm a widow?

PHILIP. Seems logical, doesn't it?

HEPZIBAH. I hadn't thought of it that way. Poor Henry! Me dead and all those girls to raise. What a time he must have had of it! *(She giggles a little)* I really oughtn't to laugh, should I? Especially when I've just found out I'm a widow. But somehow, I can't help it. My father used to say, "It'll be all the same a hundred years from now." And he's right. I just can't seem to worry about it.

PHILIP. Do you want to go back and look for the inscription? It should be on the headstone.

HEPZIBAH. Oh, no. I don't think I could. You look.

PHILIP. All right. *(He goes back and reads, mumbling. He seems surprised and glances toward Hepzibah, then returns to the bench)* Henry left this wicked world at the age of one hundred and two.

HEPZIBAH. That's just like Henry. He was a very stubborn man.

PHILIP. Well, anyway, he's gone and here we are. Probably the only two people left in the world. There's a song about that. *(He sings)* "If you were the only girl in the world, and I was the only boy..."

HEPZIBAH. What a nice voice you have! And I haven't even asked your name. I've just gone on chattering about my own troubles.

PHILIP. I'm Philip Sandford Grant, "beloved son of..." And I think I died in a car accident.

HEPZIBAH. Oh, you poor boy! What kind of an accident is that?

PHILIP. Say, that's right. I forgot you wouldn't know about that. A car is a — a — kind of wagon that runs without horses. It goes very fast.

HEPZIBAH. *(Wide-eyed)* Wouldn't it bump into things?

PHILIP. *(Ruefully)* It would. It did, I think.

HEPZIBAH. I suppose there are a lot of things I wouldn't know about?

PHILIP. Yes. Lights, telephones ... radio ... television ... jets ... space travel ... computers. Yes, lots of things.

HEPZIBAH. They sound very frightening.

PHILIP. No. They were rather nice, really. But they don't seem to be much help in a situation of this kind. We've got to figure out what we're going to do next.

HEPZIBAH. You seem like a clever boy. I'm sure you'll think of something.

PHILIP. Would you mind very much if we *were* the only people in the world?

HEPZIBAH. You know, I really don't think I would mind so very much. Of course, I expect I shall feel badly about Henry when I get around to it. But if he's been dead so long, there's not much point in that.

PHILIP. A very natural reaction, I'm sure.

HEPZIBAH. And Henry did criticize a lot. He wanted sons so badly. He was afraid the name of Jones would die out. And, of course, I wasn't much help with that. Poor Henry. He never did get his sons.

PHILIP. *(Glancing at headstone, smiling)* It must have been a great disappointment.

HEPZIBAH. What I'm really worried about are the proprieties. Henry was always very particular about the proprieties. And he wouldn't approve of my being here with you like this.

PHILIP. There's nobody left to care.

HEPZIBAH. *(Shocked)* Oh, but Philip, you mustn't talk like that. God still cares. And people who — who — well, anyway, they go to Hell.

PHILIP. But don't you see, we've missed all that. We haven't any Heaven to strive for, nor any Hell to fear. We missed the boat.

HEPZIBAH. *(Suddenly ecstatic)* Oh, Philip, wouldn't that be wonderful? We would be so — so — free!

PHILIP. That describes our case exactly.

HEPZIBAH. But we can't just live together without being married.

PHILIP. We've got to live together — we're the only ones here. And there's nobody to marry us.

HEPZIBAH. I only suggested it because of the proprieties, you know. I'm sure you wouldn't want me for a wife, anyway. *(She glances at him under her lashes)* Would you?

PHILIP. *(Laughing)* A widow 125 years old with six daughters wasn't just what I had in mind. But you're very pretty, you know, and perhaps when we know each other better....

HEPZIBAH. *(Piqued)* No, it's out of the question. Even if it were all very proper, I should never marry again. I should be faithful to Henry's memory. Henry thought second marriages were a sin.

PHILIP. *(Pricking up his ears)* Oh, he did?

HEPZIBAH. Yes. He was very strict morally, Henry was. And he did love me. He never looked at another woman.

PHILIP. *(Smiling)* He didn't?

HEPZIBAH. No. There is... *(She corrects herself)* there *was* ... a nasty red-headed young widow in our neighborhood who was always making eyes at him. A lot of good it did her!

PHILIP. What was her name?

HEPZIBAH. Jane Morrison. Why?

PHILIP. Hepzibah, I think you had better go and read your headstone.

HEPZIBAH. Why?

PHILIP. *(Smiling)* I think you had better read it.

HEPZIBAH. All right. But what's the mystery? *(She walks back and begins to read)* "Here lies Hepzibah Mercy Jones, good and devoted wife..." That's nice, isn't it? When I was alive I didn't think Henry really thought I was either good or devoted but this just shows how I misjudged him. "...of Henry Joseph Jones, who died at the birth of her sixth daughter" ...isn't that pathetic? Still I do think Henry might have said sixth child, instead of daughter. After all, there was no reason for everyone to know. "...June 1, 1884, in her twenty-fifth year..." I never did get to be thirty after all, thank goodness... "by their fruits ye shall know them." ... That's pretty. I hope he meant it as a compliment. You never could be quite sure, with Henry.

PHILIP. Read the rest.

HEPZIBAH. The next is Henry's, isn't it? "Here lies..." *(She pauses, then reads on with mounting fury)* "Jane Morrison Jones, beloved wife of Henry Joseph Jones, sainted mother of Henry, Joseph, Matthew, Anthony and James Jones, died April 25, 1932, in her seventy-fifth year. "Her household rose up and called her blessed." Oh! *(Furiously)* that red-headed viper, that scheming widow, that black-hearted, unprincipled, two-faced, conniving snake! She married him! The minute my back was turned, she married him! Before I was cold in the grave, she was over there, petting my little girls, baking those biscuits she was so proud of, setting bread in my tins, sleeping on my feather tick... Oh! Oh!

PHILIP. You said Henry thought second marriages were sinful.

HEPZIBAH. *(Coming downstage to Philip)* He did. He told me so, time and time again. But she — she — enticed him, that's what she did. Oh, such wickedness!

PHILIP. And she'd been married before, too. Old Henry committed a double dipper.

HEPZIBAH. *(Sniffling)* And sons. She had five sons. And he put all their names on the headstone, every one. And not one of my girls, not a single one. And they had such pretty names, too. Violet, Rose, Lily, Faith and Hope. I was going to name the last one Charity. And now I don't even know what they named her. Jane, probably.

PHILIP. *(Pulling her down to bench)* Hepzibah, why don't you be sensible about this? What's the use of getting all worked up. Jane's dead long ago and so's Henry and we've got the laugh on both of them. So why don't we just make the best of it? *(He puts his arm around her and she puts her head on his shoulder)*

HEPZIBAH. Oh, Philip, you're such a comfort to me. I'm so glad it was you I got resurrected with.

PHILIP. And I'm glad I got you instead of Jane. She was 75.

HEPZIBAH. *(Cheered)* You're so sweet, Philip. I feel as if I'd known you always and always.

PHILIP. And if I'd known you were here, I'd have brought you flowers every Sunday. *(They lean toward each other. They almost kiss. But...)*

HEPZIBAH. *(Suddenly)* Philip, do you know something?

PHILIP. What is it?

HEPZIBAH. I've never told anyone before.

PHILIP. *(Tenderly)* You can tell me.

HEPZIBAH. *(In a sudden burst)* Henry was a mean, nasty, bad-tempered old hypocrite!

PHILIP. I thought so, all the time.

HEPZIBAH. And there's something else.

PHILIP. Get it off your chest.

HEPZIBAH. He was going bald.

PHILIP. I knew it! I was sure of it!

HEPZIBAH. I don't know what Jane Morrison saw in him.

PHILIP. Atta girl, Hepzibah!

HEPZIBAH. Papa made me marry him. He had a nice farm and Papa respected him and nobody cared what I thought.

PHILIP. *(Patting her hand)* Poor little Hepzibah.

HEPZIBAH. And Philip, I lied to him. I didn't try to have boys. I prayed every time they'd be girls. I prayed and prayed.

PHILIP. Good for you!

HEPZIBAH. And Henry prayed and prayed for boys.

PHILIP. But you won.

HEPZIBAH. Yes, and that proves something, doesn't it? I was afraid my luck would run out, though. So perhaps it's just as well I died.

PHILIP. It was a lucky break for me, anyway.

HEPZIBAH. Weren't you ever married, Philip?

PHILIP. Not ... exactly.

HEPZIBAH. Philip!!

PHILIP. *(Hastily)* I mean, it didn't really come to anything. Not really, you know. I think I must have been waiting for you.

HEPZIBAH. *(Dreamily)* It's funny the way we met, isn't it?

PHILIP. That's the world's biggest understatement.

HEPZIBAH. You'll think I'm silly, but I'm beginning to be glad we didn't hear that old horn.

PHILIP. I was glad from the first moment I saw you getting up in your funny little hat. *(They lean toward each other. They almost kiss. But...)*

HEPZIBAH. *(Suddenly)* Philip, do you suppose we'll get hungry?

PHILIP. I've been trying not to think about that.

HEPZIBAH. Or sleepy?

PHILIP. I don't think I'd dare go to sleep. I can't be trusted to wake up when the alarm goes off.

HEPZIBAH. And do you really think everyone is dead?

PHILIP. There's certainly nobody home in these parts, anyway.

HEPZIBAH. Let's not stay here. It isn't very cheerful.

PHILIP. No, we'll have to scout around. But I'm not too keen on taking a look at the town dressed like this, just in case. Perhaps you could go?

HEPZIBAH. In my nightgown?

PHILIP. Well, you look more like a ghost than I do.

HEPZIBAH. Oh, Philip, I feel so ashamed dressed like this. Please don't go on teasing me about it.

PHILIP. I think you look sweet.

HEPZIBAH. Henry and I were married seven years, and he never once told me I was sweet.

PHILIP. *(Leaning close to her)* I can say lots of things Henry never said...

HEPZIBAH. Shall we stay here until it gets dark?

PHILIP. We might even stay *awhile* after dark. *(At the upstage right, an old man hobbles in with a cane. He makes his way slowly across to the center gravel walk and down toward Hepzibah and Philip. They are oblivious)*

HEPZIBAH. Philip, do you know something? I think 1984 is more fun than 1884 was.

PHILIP. I'm kinda partial to it myself. *(They kiss, then join in a warm embrace and a longer kiss, oblivious of their surroundings. HENRY enters. He is a wizened, bald old man, carrying a cane, his voice cracked with age. He looks every year of 102. He wears a suit of what is known as rusty black, shiny, creased and worn at the cuffs. He has a white wing collar and black tie, boots that lace above the ankle.)*

HENRY. HEPZIBAH! *(The lovers leap apart but turn toward him, still holding hands)*

HEPZIBAH. Who are you?

PHILIP. Could you possibly be...?

HENRY. Hepzibah, stop this nonsense. I'm Henry and you know it. What are you a-doin' there? Who's this young scoundrel with you? Answer me!

PHILIP. Henry! Well, if it isn't old Henry Joseph Jones himself.

HEPZIBAH. Oh Henry, is that really you? You look so funny!

HENRY. Funny, eh? And how do you look, you shameless hussy! And where have you been? Didn't you hear the horn? And who is this young fellow without his clothes on? Where did you dig him up, eh? *(JANE is entering back-*

stage right, coming across to center gravel walk and down toward the others. She is dressed in severe black. She wears a cameo at her throat. She appears prim and conventional in every respect)

PHILIP and HEPZIBAH. *(Together)* The horn. What horn?

HENRY. Gabriel's Horn. It's the Day. It's the Great Getting Up Morning. They sent me back to find you. Get a move on, girl.

HEPZIBAH. I'm not coming.

PHILIP. She doesn't have to go with you.

HENRY. She's my wife. I'm responsible for her. Our girls will be waitin'. Come on, Hepzibah, and don't keep me standin' here all day. *(He tries to hook her with cane)*

HEPZIBAH. *(Backing away)* Oh, no! I don't like you. I never liked you. Go away.

PHILIP. *(Quoting)* "You're a mean, nasty, bad-tempered old hypocrite. And besides, you're bald!"

HENRY. Why, you young whipper-snapper! *(He shakes cane at him)*

JANE. Henry! *(She is nearly upon them)*

HEPZIBAH. *(Looking)* That's Jane Morrison's cackle, sure as I'm born. Now you listen to me, Henry Jones, I know all about what you did. You married Jane Morrison and you can't deny it. It's right there *(Pointing to headstone)* in graven stone! So you can just go to Glory with *her*. *I'm* not coming with you.

JANE. Henry Jones, what's keeping you? Well, Hepzibah, a fine sight you look, I must say. I told Henry to bury you in your black alpaca, but no, he had to bury you in a nightgown. Now see what's come of it.

HEPZIBAH. I can see plain enough what's come of you,

Jane Morrison! You're as grey as an old goose and as wrinkled as a prune. Where's that fancy red hair of yours now, I'd like to know?

HENRY. Now, Hepzibah, don't you talk to Jane like that. She's my second wife, good and proper, and you treat her respectful like.

HEPZIBAH. Good and proper, eh? Changed your mind about second marriages, didn't you. Well, she's your wife and you can have her. Nobody else *(With a smug glance at Philip)* wants her, I'm sure. But you're not having me, too, so you just hobble back with her.

PHILIP. *(Shouting)* Bravo, Hepzibah!

JANE. There now, Henry, didn't I tell you? Such a mealy-mouthed little thing she used to pretend to be. Butter wouldn't melt in her mouth. It was "Yes Henry" this and "Yes Henry" that. But I saw through her, all right! I told you she was a spiteful little piece, and so she is.

HEPZIBAH. Nobody needs to tell me what a ninny I was! If I hadn't been such ... a ... a mouse I'd have had my hands in that red hair of yours many a time. Getting Henry for a second husband serves you good and right. You can just keep him. I don't know where any of us are going, but I'm going with Philip.

HENRY. Saints preserve us, girl, I don't know what's got into you. Being dead so long hasn't improved you a bit. But I'm not standing here any longer listening to a woman's wrangle. I'm not so young as I used to be and I'd better be gettin' on back. It's nearly time for the sheep and goats to get divided and I'm not losing my place in line for a couple of bickering females. Now, Jane, let's get along. Hepzibah can do as she pleases.

JANE. Hepzibah generally does. But you'd think she'd want to see her girls again. I just can't hardly wait to see my boys.

HEPZIBAH. You're mighty uppity about those boys, aren't you, Jane Morrison? Pesky, dirty things, boys are. I wouldn't give them houseroom.

JANE. Sour grapes! *(Sneering)* Seems like you're mighty fond of one boy anyway. And he doesn't appear to be any better than he should be. *(To Philip)* What are you hiding down here for, young man, 'stead of going on into Judgment like any decent body would?

PHILIP. Is anybody looking for me up there?

HENRY. There's a list of deserters up there on the Judgment Bulletin Board as long as your arm. What's your name, young feller?

PHILIP. Philip Sandford Grant.

HENRY. Grant, you say?

PHILIP. Yes.

HENRY. Philip Sandford Grant. What might your father's name be?

PHILIP. John Sandford Grant.

HENRY. H'm. And your grandfather, now. What might his name be?

PHILIP. He was William Sandford Grant. *(HENRY cackles with laughter. He pounds his cane. He doubles up. He slaps Jane on the back, then cackles on, pounding his knee. JANE begins to laugh. She rocks back and forth, pointing a finger at Hepzibah and Philip, then going off into further gales of helpless laughter. PHILIP and HEPZIBAH stare at the other two in amazement. They look at each other questioningly, then back at the laughing old man and woman)*

PHILIP. *(Coldly)* We're glad to be so amusing. But would you mind telling us the joke?

HEPZIBAH. *(Grimly)* It's bound to be something horrid or he wouldn't be laughing. *(She points to Henry)*

HENRY. *(Struggling not to laugh, gasping and choking)* Why, Hepzibah, do you know who that young feller is? He's your great-great grandson, that's who he is. And you were getting sweet on him. You're his great-great grandmother. *(He slaps Jane a resounding whack, points at Hepzibah, and chortles)* Kissin' him, she was. Arms wrapped around each other like sweethearts. Saw 'em with my own eyes. Cuddlin' and courtin'. And she's his great-great-grandmother! Oh, I'll die laughin'. *(He laughs again. HEPZIBAH and PHILIP are stunned. They have been looking at each other in horror during this speech. PHILIP backs away from Hepzibah. She puts out a hand to him, then drops it sadly to her side. She turns fiercly on Henry and Jane)*

HEPZIBAH. You're making it up! It's not true. You're both of you lying! I didn't have any grandchildren, let alone great-great grandchildren. You made it up.

JANE. *(Sarcastically)* S'pose the whole world came to an end when you died, Hepzibah! What do you think your little girls did? They grew up, that's what they did! And your youngest, Charity, we named her, she married Sandford Grant, as handsome a young man as ever I did see. Favored this young man, he did. *(Pointing to Philip)* And their oldest boy was William Sandford Grant and he got married and had a little shaver named John. John Sandford Grant. This young man's father. I remember that baby as plain as day. Biggest ears I ever saw on a baby!

PHILIP. *(Stricken)* That was Dad all right!

HEPZIBAH. Oh, Philip, and I said I felt as if I'd known you for years. And to think my own little Charity did this to me. Oh, Oh! *(She weeps)*

PHILIP. *(Patting her shoulder)* Don't cry *(Long pause)* ... Grandmother.

HEPZIBAH. *(To Henry)* And you did call her Charity after all?

HENRY. Yes, Hepzibah, I did. It was your dyin' wish and I respected it. She was the prettiest of all the girls. Just the image of you, my dear.

HEPZIBAH. *(With a fierce look at Jane)* And Henry, you didn't let any of those rough boys of Jane's tease her, did you?

JANE. *(Snappishly)* If you live to be a hundred, you'll never get over my having those boys, will you?

HENRY. *(Ignoring her)* No sir, I didn't, Hepzibah. I surely didn't. Young Henry pulled her ringlets one day — long, black ringlets she had. I always did like black hair *(Jane sniffs again)* and I marched him right out to the woodshed. Tanned him good.

HEPZIBAH. *(Gratefully)* Thank you Henry, *(The Trumpet sounds. A quick series of rising notes, imperative in tone)*

HENRY. Land o'Goshen, Gabriel's gettin mad. Come on, Jane. *(JANE takes his arm, tosses her head at Hepzibah, and they make their way slowly up the path and out. PHILIP and HEPZIBAH look at each other. Then PHILIP bows before her with a flourish, kisses her hand and offers her his arm. She curtsies deeply and takes his arm.*

PHILIP. Come, Grandmother. The sheep are gone. And it's beginning to look as if we're the goats! *(They march off as — The Curtain Falls.)*

MUSIC USE NOTE

Licensees are solely responsible for obtaining formal written permission from copyright owners to use copyrighted music in the performance of this play and are strongly cautioned to do so. If no such permission is obtained by the licensee, then the licensee must use only original music that the licensee owns and controls. Licensees are solely responsible and liable for all music clearances and shall indemnify the copyright owners of the play(s) and their licensing agent, Samuel French, against any costs, expenses, losses and liabilities arising from the use of music by licensees. Please contact the appropriate music licensing authority in your territory for the rights to any incidental music.

IMPORTANT BILLING AND CREDIT REQUIREMENTS

If you have obtained performance rights to this title, please refer to your licensing agreement for important billing and credit requirements.

www.ingramcontent.com/pod-product-compliance
Lightning Source LLC
Chambersburg PA
CBHW052000290426
44110CB00015B/2320